New York
The Empire State

Tika Downey

PowerKiDS press™

New York

Published in 2010 by The Rosen Publishing Group, Inc.
29 East 21st Street, New York, NY 10010

First Edition

Editor: Joanne Randolph
Book Design: Greg Tucker
Photo Researcher: Jessica Gerweck

Photo Credits: Cover, pp. 5, 13 (main), 13 (inset), 17, 19, 22 (tree), 22 (bird), 22 (flower) Shutterstock. com; p. 7 © SuperStock, Inc./SuperStock; p. 9 Phillippe Bourseiller/Getty Images; p. 11 James Hager/ Getty Images; p. 15 © Alan Schein Photography/Corbis; p. 22 (animal) © www.istockphoto.com/Simon Phipps; p. 22 (Theodore Roosevelt and Alex Rodriguez) Getty Images; p. 22 (Jennifer Lopez) Getty Images for IMG.

Library of Congress Cataloging-in-Publication Data

Downey, Tika.
  New York : the Empire State / Tika Downey. — 1st ed.
       p. cm. — (Our amazing states)
  Includes index.
  ISBN 978-1-4042-8108-0 (library binding) — ISBN 978-1-4358-3336-4 (pbk.) —
ISBN 978-1-4358-3337-1 (6-pack)
  1. New York (State)—Juvenile literature. I. Title.
  F119.3.D69 2010
  974.7—dc22
                                                2008055827

Manufactured in the United States of America

Contents

The Empire State   4

A Trip Through Time   6

From the Hudson River to Niagara Falls   8

New York's Wild Side   10

Making Money   12

All Around Albany   14

The Big Apple   16

Lady Liberty   18

There's No Place Quite Like It   20

Glossary   21

New York State at a Glance   22

Index   24

Web Sites   24

The Empire State

Almost everyone has heard of New York. It is an important center of business, finance, and the arts, in the northeastern United States. George Washington, the first U.S. president, once called New York the capital of the **empire**. That may be how New York got its nickname, the Empire State.

When people think of New York, they often picture the crowded streets and **skyscrapers** of New York City. Yet the state is also famous for its lakes, forests, mountains, and natural wonders such as Niagara Falls. Whether you like the city or the country, New York has something for you!

New York City is home to millions of people, with millions more visiting the city each year. This picture shows Manhattan Island, which is part of New York City.

The first people in New York were Native Americans, who arrived about 11,000 years ago. Thousands of years later, Europeans and other people came to New York, too.

Dutch settlers came in the early 1600s and founded a **colony** called New Netherland. The English took over the colony in 1664 and changed the name to New York.

Between 1775 and 1783, many battles were fought in New York during the **American Revolution**. Through this war, the colonies gained their freedom from Britain and formed the United States. New York became the country's eleventh state on July 26, 1788.

New Netherland was a busy place. Here supplies are being unloaded from ships and people have come to trade for the things they need.

From the Hudson River to Niagara Falls

New York is known for its natural beauty, which includes mountains, rivers, and lakes. The Catskill Mountains, Adirondack Mountains, and Hudson River lie in eastern New York. The long, thin Finger Lakes are in central New York. You can also visit the huge and powerful Niagara Falls in New York. This waterfall is one of the world's natural wonders.

New York's weather is generally warm in summer and cold in winter. Spring is often rainy. Winter may bring lots of snow. For example, Syracuse gets about 9.5 feet (3 m) of snow every year!

The force of Niagara Falls' water makes 4 million kilowatts of power for New York and Canada.

New York's Wild Side

Did you know that forests cover more than half of New York? These forests are filled with many kinds of trees, from evergreens to sweet gum and sugar maple trees. Woodpeckers, geese, owls, and other birds fill the fields and forests. There are deer, raccoons, porcupines, foxes, and bears, too.

You might see beaver **lodges** in the rivers and lakes. The beaver is New York's state animal. It has soft fur, a paddle-shaped tail, and strong front teeth, which it uses to cut down trees. Beavers are excellent swimmers and can hold their breath under water for 15 minutes!

This beaver is chewing on a plant along a river's edge. Beavers are herbivores, which means they eat only plants.

Making Money

New York has all kinds of businesses. Have you ever heard of Wall Street? It is New York City's famous banking and business center. The city also has companies that produce books, clothes, movies, and TV shows.

New York has factories that make everything from makeup to computer parts. Your toothpaste, the paint on your house, or the canned vegetables you had for dinner might have been made in New York!

New York also has lots of farms. These farms produce milk and all sorts of fruits and vegetables. Apples are the top fruit crop in the state.

This farm is in Pine Island, New York, which is known for its rich, black soil. *Inset:* The New York Stock Exchange, in New York City, is the world's largest stock exchange.

All Around Albany

Albany has been the capital of New York since 1797. It is also one of the nation's oldest cities. Dutch **colonists** built the first settlement there in 1624.

One of Albany's most famous sights is an oval building called the Egg. Other famous buildings include the state capitol, which looks a little like a French castle, and several huge homes built for rich families in the late 1700s.

You can see art, clothes, furniture, and other objects from New York's past at the Albany **Institute** of History and Art. Some of the objects there are over 300 years old!

The Egg houses Albany's performing arts center. It took 12 years to build the center, but it was finally ready for use in 1978.

The Big Apple

New York City, which is often called the Big Apple, is the largest city in the United States. More than eight million people live there! Dutch colonists built the first settlement there in 1625. Since then people have come from around the world to live in the city. New York City is made up of five boroughs, or neighborhoods. These are Manhattan, the Bronx, Brooklyn, Queens, and Staten Island.

More than 30 million people visit New York City every year. They come to see its skyscrapers, beautiful old buildings, and Central Park. They come to shop, see plays on Broadway, and visit art **museums**. There is so much to see and do that there is never enough time!

This is a view of Manhattan. The tall building on the left is the Empire State Building, which is one of the buildings many people come to see.

Lady Liberty

Have you ever heard of a giant, green woman who is 152 feet (46 m) tall? One of New York City's most famous sights is the **Statue** of **Liberty**. This huge statue is a figure of a woman in a long dress and crown. In her right hand, she holds a lit torch. In her left hand, she holds a book with the date of the **Declaration of Independence** on it.

France gave the statue to the United States as a sign of the friendship between the two countries. The statue was finished in 1884 and put in place in 1886. Today, the Statue of Liberty is known around the world. Millions of people visit it each year.

The Statue of Liberty arrived in New York's harbor in 1885, in 350 pieces. The statue was not put together until 1886, though.

There's No Place Quite Like It

As you can see, there is so much you can do in New York! You can visit wonderful, busy New York City. You can see the **government** at work in Albany or visit the Baseball Hall of Fame, in Cooperstown. There are also many places where you can learn about the history and importance of the Erie **Canal**, including the Erie Canal Museum, in Syracuse, the Canal Town Museum, in Canastota, or the Erie Canal Village, in Rome.

In spring and summer, you can climb mountains, swim in lakes, or go boating. In fall, you can view brightly colored trees. In winter, you can go skiing in the mountains. What would you like to do in New York?

Glossary

American Revolution (uh-MER-ih-ken reh-vuh-LOO-shun) The war between the colonies and Britain that resulted in the United States becoming its own country.

canal (ka-NAL) A man-made waterway.

colonists (KAH-luh-nists) People who live in a colony.

colony (KAH-luh-nee) A new place where people move that is still ruled by the leaders of the country from which they came.

Declaration of Independence (deh-kluh-RAY-shun UV in-duh-PEN-dints) An official announcement signed on July 4, 1776, in which American colonists stated they were free of British rule.

empire (EM-pyr) A large area controlled by one ruler.

government (GUH-vern-mint) The people who make laws and run a state or a country.

institute (IN-stih-toot) A group, such as a school or museum, that teaches people about a certain subject.

liberty (LIH-ber-tee) Freedom.

lodges (LOJ-iz) Homes for certain animals.

museums (myoo-ZEE-umz) Places where art or historical pieces are safely kept for people to see and to study.

skyscrapers (SKY-skray-perz) Very tall buildings.

statue (STA-chyoo) An image of a person or an animal, generally cut in clay, metal, or stone.

New York State Symbols

State Tree
Sugar Maple

State Animal
Beaver

State Flag

State Bird
Bluebird

State Flower
Rose

State Seal

Famous People from New York

Elizabeth Cady Stanton
(1815–1902)
Born in Johnstown, NY
Suffragist/Women's
Rights Activist

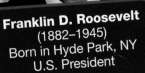

Franklin D. Roosevelt
(1882–1945)
Born in Hyde Park, NY
U.S. President

Maurice Sendak
(1928–)
Born in Brooklyn, NY
Writer/Illustrator

New York State Map

Legend

○ Major City

✪ Capital

〜 River

Lake Champlain

St. Lawrence River

Adirondack Mountains

Saratoga Springs ○

Lake Ontario

Mohawk River

Albany ✪

Rochester ○

○ Syracuse

Niagara Falls

Finger Lakes

Catskill Mountains

Hudson River

○ Buffalo

Lake Erie

Long Island

New York City ○

New York State Facts

Population: 19,297,729

Area: About 49,576 square miles (128,401 sq km)

Motto: Excelsior, "Ever Upward"

Song: "I Love New York," words and music by Steve Karmen

A
Albany, 14, 23
art(s), 4, 14

B
Baseball Hall of Fame, 20
beaver(s), 10, 22
Big Apple, 16
Broadway, 16
business(es), 4, 12

C
Catskill Mountains, 8
Central Park, 16

D
deer, 10
Dutch settlers, 6, 14

E
Egg, 14
Erie Canal, 20

F
factories, 12
farms, 12
Finger Lakes, 8
forests, 4, 10

G
geese, 10

H
Hudson River, 8

L
lakes, 4, 8, 20

N
Native Americans, 6
New Netherland, 6
Niagara Falls, 4, 8

S
skiing, 20
skyscrapers, 4, 16
Statue of Liberty, 18
sugar maple trees, 10, 22
Syracuse, 8

T
TV shows, 12

W
Wall Street, 12
woodpeckers, 10

Web Sites

Due to the changing nature of Internet links, PowerKids Press has developed an online list of Web sites related to the subject of this book. This site is updated regularly. Please use this link to access the list:

www.powerkidslinks.com/amst/ny/